MANCINI MAGIC

Photo appears courtesy of the Henry Mancini estate.

— PIANO LEVEL —
LATE INTERMEDIATE/EARLY ADVANCED

ISBN 978-1-61774-051-0

HAL•LEONARD® CORPORATION

7777 W. BLUEMOUND RD. P.O. BOX 13819 MILWAUKEE, WI 53213

Visit Hal Leonard Online at
www.halleonard.com

PREFACE

Henry Mancini is one of my musical heroes. I studied his creations very carefully during my developmental years as a young composer and arranger. I consider his output to embody some of the finest examples of commercial writing from the 20th century. Mr. Mancini did it all with consummate good taste: songwriting, arranging, orchestrating, conducting... and he had a magical touch at the piano as well.

This collection includes some of his most successful compositions, as well as a few of his lesser-known works that are among my personal favorites. In the process of arranging these pieces, I took the opportunity to listen (and re-listen) to many of Mancini's recordings. The experience was both inspiring and educational. I remain a devoted fan!

Sincerely,
Phillip Keveren

P.S. The photograph on the cover was shot circa 1970. That was right when I was first discovering Henry Mancini's music. I spent many hours at the piano trying to decipher the harmonies in "The Pink Panther." Thanks for the music, Mr. Mancini!

◆

BIOGRAPHY

Phillip Keveren, a multi-talented keyboard artist and composer, has composed original works in a variety of genres from piano solo to symphonic orchestra. Mr. Keveren gives frequent concerts and workshops for teachers and their students in the United States, Canada, Europe, and Asia. Mr. Keveren holds a B.M. in composition from California State University Northridge and a M.M. in composition from the University of Southern California.

CONTENTS

BABY ELEPHANT WALK
from the Paramount Picture HATARI!

By HENRY MANCINI
Arranged by Phillip Keveren

CRAZY WORLD
from VICTOR/VICTORIA

Lyrics by LESLIE BRICUSSE
Music by HENRY MANCINI
Arranged by Phillip Keveren

CHARADE
Theme from the Film CHARADE

By HENRY MANCINI
Arranged by Phillip Keveren

DAYS OF WINE AND ROSES
Theme from the Film DAYS OF WINE AND ROSES

Lyric by JOHNNY MERCER
Music by HENRY MANCINI
Arranged by Phillip Keveren

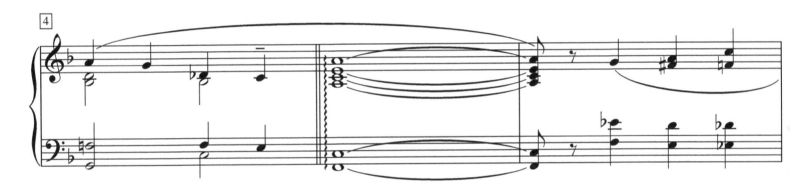

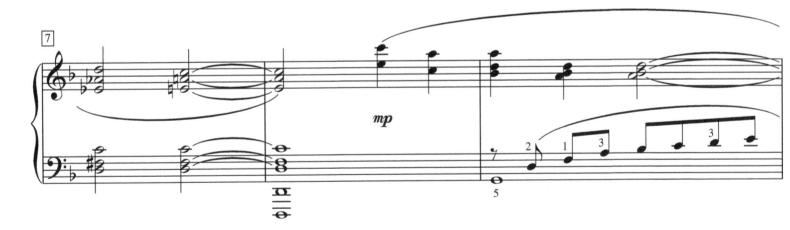

DEAR HEART
Theme from the Film DEAR HEART

By HENRY MANCINI
Arranged by Phillip Keveren

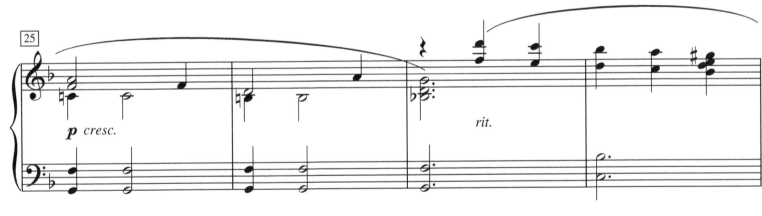

DREAMSVILLE
from the TV Series PETER GUNN

By HENRY MANCINI
Arranged by Phillip Keveren

Tenderly (♩ = 84–92)

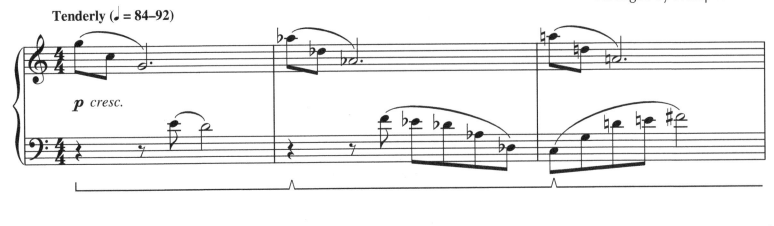

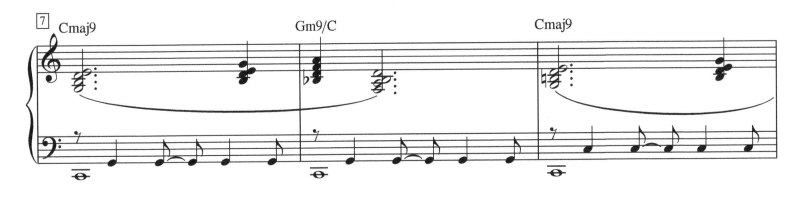

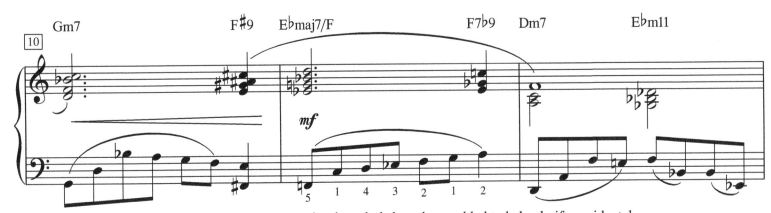

Due to the chromatic nature of this arrangement, chord symbols have been added to help clarify accidentals.

MR. LUCKY
Theme from the TV Series MR. LUCKY

By HENRY MANCINI
Arranged by Phillip Keveren

Smooth Latin groove (♩ = 126)

HOW SOON
Theme from the TV Show THE RICHARD BOONE SHOW

Words by AL STILLMAN
Music by HENRY MANCINI
Arranged by Phillip Keveren

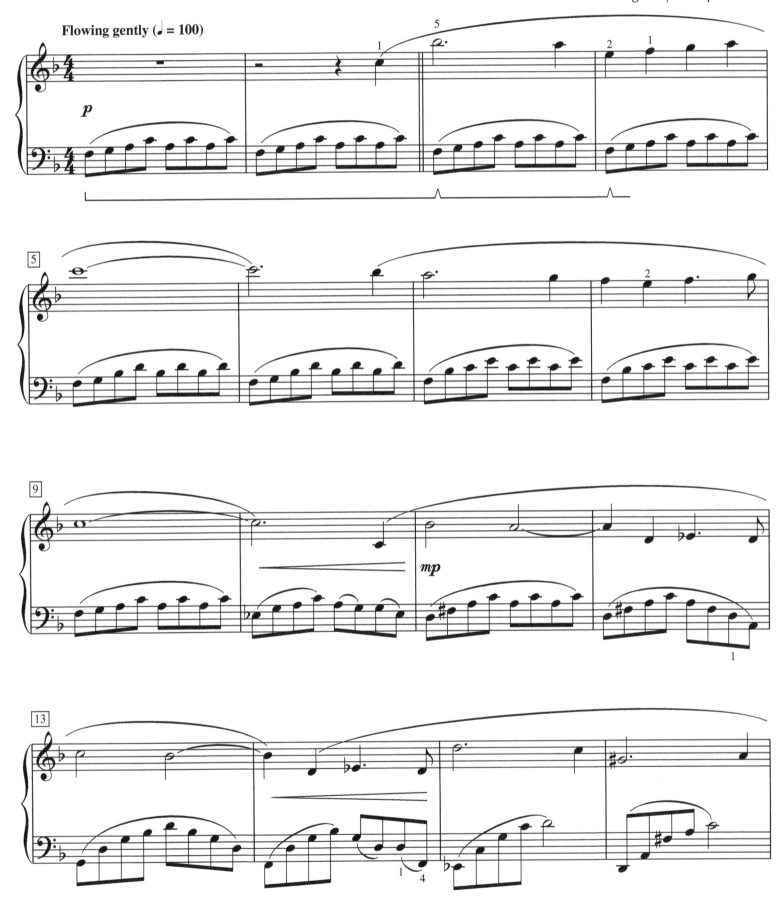

MOMENT TO MOMENT
Theme from the Film MOMENT TO MOMENT

By HENRY MANCINI
Arranged by Phillip Keveren

MOON RIVER
from the Paramount Picture BREAKFAST AT TIFFANY'S

Words by JOHNNY MERCER
Music by HENRY MANCINI
Arranged by Phillip Keveren

Tenderly (♩ = 92)

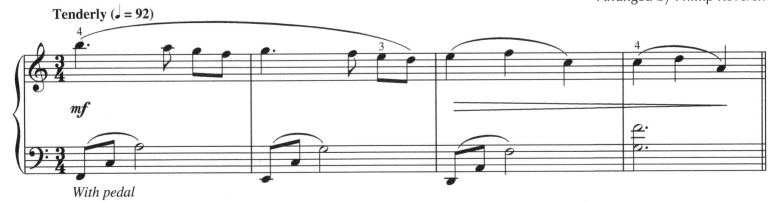

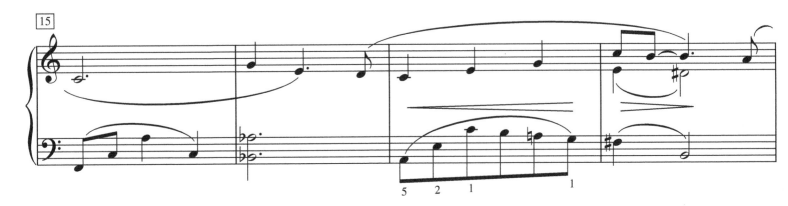

PETER GUNN
Theme Song from The Television Series

By HENRY MANCINI
Arranged by Phillip Keveren

THE PINK PANTHER
Theme from the Film THE PINK PANTHER

By HENRY MANCINI
Arranged by Phillip Keveren

THE THORN BIRDS
(Main Theme)
from the TV Miniseries THE THORN BIRDS

By HENRY MANCINI
Arranged by Phillip Keveren

TWO FOR THE ROAD
Theme from the Film TWO FOR THE ROAD

Music by HENRY MANCINI
Words by LESLIE BRICUSSE
Arranged by Phillip Keveren

WHISTLING AWAY THE DARK
from the Film DARLING LILI

Words by JOHNNY MERCER
Music by HENRY MANCINI
Arranged by Phillip Keveren

THE PHILLIP KEVEREN SERIES

PIANO SOLO

ABBA FOR CLASSICAL PIANO
00156644..$14.99

ABOVE ALL
00311024..$12.99

BACH MEETS JAZZ
00198473..$14.99

THE BEATLES
00306412..$16.99

THE BEATLES FOR CLASSICAL PIANO
00312189..$14.99

THE BEATLES – RECITAL SUITES
00275876..$19.99

BEST PIANO SOLOS
00312546..$14.99

BLESSINGS
00156601..$12.99

BLUES CLASSICS
00198656..$12.99

BROADWAY'S BEST
00310669..$14.99

A CELTIC CHRISTMAS
00310629..$12.99

THE CELTIC COLLECTION
00310549..$12.95

CELTIC SONGS WITH A CLASSICAL FLAIR
00280571..$12.99

CHRISTMAS MEDLEYS
00311414..$12.99

CHRISTMAS AT THE MOVIES
00312190..$14.99

CHRISTMAS SONGS FOR CLASSICAL PIANO
00233788..$12.99

CINEMA CLASSICS
00310607..$14.99

CLASSICAL JAZZ
00311083..$12.95

COLDPLAY FOR CLASSICAL PIANO
00137779..$15.99

DISNEY RECITAL SUITES
00249097..$16.99

DISNEY SONGS FOR CLASSICAL PIANO
00311754..$16.99

DISNEY SONGS FOR RAGTIME PIANO
00241379..$16.99

THE FILM SCORE COLLECTION
00311811..$14.99

FOLKSONGS WITH A CLASSICAL FLAIR
00269408..$12.99

GOLDEN SCORES
00233789..$14.99

GOSPEL GREATS
00144351..$12.99

GREAT STANDARDS
00311157..$12.95

THE HYMN COLLECTION
00311071..$12.99

HYMN MEDLEYS
00311349..$12.99

HYMNS IN A CELTIC STYLE
00280705..$12.99

HYMNS WITH A CLASSICAL FLAIR
00269407..$12.99

HYMNS WITH A TOUCH OF JAZZ
00311249..$12.99

JINGLE JAZZ
00310762..$14.99

BILLY JOEL FOR CLASSICAL PIANO
00175310..$15.99

ELTON JOHN FOR CLASSICAL PIANO
00126449..$15.99

LET FREEDOM RING!
00310839..$12.99

ANDREW LLOYD WEBBER
00313227..$15.99

MANCINI MAGIC
00313523..$14.99

MORE DISNEY SONGS FOR CLASSICAL PIANO
00312113..$15.99

MOTOWN HITS
00311295..$12.95

PIAZZOLLA TANGOS
00306870..$15.99

QUEEN FOR CLASSICAL PIANO
00156645..$15.99

RICHARD RODGERS CLASSICS
00310755..$15.99

SHOUT TO THE LORD!
00310699..$14.99

SONGS FROM CHILDHOOD FOR EASY CLASSICAL PIANO
00233688..$12.99

THE SOUND OF MUSIC
00119403..$14.99

SYMPHONIC HYMNS FOR PIANO
00224738..$14.99

TIN PAN ALLEY
00279673..$12.99

TREASURED HYMNS FOR CLASSICAL PIANO
00312112..$14.99

THE TWELVE KEYS OF CHRISTMAS
00144926..$12.99

YULETIDE JAZZ
00311911..$17.99

EASY PIANO

AFRICAN-AMERICAN SPIRITUALS
00310610..$10.99

CATCHY SONGS FOR PIANO
00218387..$12.99

CELTIC DREAMS
00310973..$10.95

CHRISTMAS CAROLS FOR EASY CLASSICAL PIANO
00233686..$12.99

CHRISTMAS POPS
00311126..$14.99

CLASSIC POP/ROCK HITS
00311548..$12.95

A CLASSICAL CHRISTMAS
00310769..$10.95

CLASSICAL MOVIE THEMES
00310975..$12.99

CONTEMPORARY WORSHIP FAVORITES
00311805..$14.99

DISNEY SONGS FOR EASY CLASSICAL PIANO
00144352..$12.99

EARLY ROCK 'N' ROLL
00311093..$12.99

GEORGE GERSHWIN CLASSICS
00110374..$12.99

GOSPEL TREASURES
00310805..$12.99

THE VINCE GUARALDI COLLECTION
00306821..$16.99

HYMNS FOR EASY CLASSICAL PIANO
00160294..$12.99

IMMORTAL HYMNS
00310798..$12.99

JAZZ STANDARDS
00311294..$12.99

LOVE SONGS
00310744..$12.99

THE MOST BEAUTIFUL SONGS FOR EASY CLASSICAL PIANO
00233740..$12.99

POP STANDARDS FOR EASY CLASSICAL PIANO
00233739..$12.99

RAGTIME CLASSICS
00311293..$10.95

SONGS FROM CHILDHOOD FOR EASY CLASSICAL PIANO
00233688..$12.99

SONGS OF INSPIRATION
00103258..$12.99

TIMELESS PRAISE
00310712..$12.95

10,000 REASONS
00126450..$14.99

TV THEMES
00311086..$12.99

21 GREAT CLASSICS
00310717..$12.99

WEEKLY WORSHIP
00145342..$16.99

BIG-NOTE PIANO

CHILDREN'S FAVORITE MOVIE SONGS
00310838..$12.99

CHRISTMAS MUSIC
00311247..$10.95

CLASSICAL FAVORITES
00277368..$12.99

CONTEMPORARY HITS
00310907..$12.99

DISNEY FAVORITES
00277370..$14.99

JOY TO THE WORLD
00310888..$10.95

THE NUTCRACKER
00310908..$10.99

STAR WARS
00277371..$16.99

BEGINNING PIANO SOLOS

AWESOME GOD
00311202..$12.99

CHRISTIAN CHILDREN'S FAVORITES
00310837..$12.99

CHRISTMAS FAVORITES
00311246..$10.95

CHRISTMAS TIME IS HERE
00311334..$12.99

CHRISTMAS TRADITIONS
00311117..$10.99

EASY HYMNS
00311250..$12.99

EVERLASTING GOD
00102710..$10.99

JAZZY TUNES
00311403..$10.95

PIANO DUET

CLASSICAL THEME DUETS
00311350..$10.99

HYMN DUETS
00311544..$12.99

PRAISE & WORSHIP DUETS
00311203..$12.99

STAR WARS
00119405..$14.99

WORSHIP SONGS FOR TWO
00253545..$12.99

HAL•LEONARD®

Visit **www.halleonard.com**
for a complete series listing.

Prices, contents, and availability subject to change without notice.

0419
158